Poems That Move You

Inspirational Poetry

by

Following Whispers

Chapter and Verse Publishing

Copyright © 2019 Clinton Burns

First published in 2019

by Chapter and Verse Publishing

All Rights Reserved. No part of this book may be reproduced in any format, print or electronic, without explicit permission in writing from the copyright owner.

ISBN 978-1-9164627-2-4

To find out more about the author, this publication or their other available offerings, please go to:

followingwhispers.com

Dedication

This book is dedicated to my loved ones who are no longer here, thank you for watching over me, guiding me, and inspiring me, as I continue to realise my dream of reaching people through my writing; entertaining them with my poems; and making this World a better, more understanding and loving place in the process. I miss you all so much, and I hope that in my deeds, I am making you proud, and honouring this gift of life I've been given.

Contents

Introduction: Something Different	1
Crazy Belief • Captive-elated	4
No Laughing Matter • Dreams	5
Within • Serendipity	6
Dauntless • Guilty	7
Onwards • Wonderment • Wormhole Goal	8
Star Of The Show • Space To Swing • Moon Gazing	9
Hero • Flow • Hole Heartedly	10
Bituminous • Soul-Do-Yours	11
Decisively Foggy • Love Locked • Know Regrets	12
Pivotal Pursuit • Boldly Go • Upwards	13
Magic's Cost • Drops 'n' Ducks • Pack	14
Hopeful • Remember	15
Puppy Love • Solid, Dependable • Enlighten-meant	16
Love-aluate • My Sunshine • Chosen	17
Quiver • Together • Lively	18
Stop Stopping • Leap • Determined	19
Heart-istry • Cirque Du So-Feel • Cogitate	20
Clocked • Innocence • Fruitful	21

Thank You • Secure • Ten Out Of Tennis	22
Bwaver-wee • Resonance	23
Avenged • Game On	24
Rewardzzz • Steep Odds	25
Beyond • Useful	26
Aq-we-us • Swimathon	27
Titillated • Combust	28
Firewalker • Pow Wow	29
Paradox • Ruffled	30
No I In • Deep	31
Poison • Internalise	32
Alarming • Philanthropy	33
Hissstory • Would They?	34
Farewell • Lonely Hollow	35
Restitution • Catalyst	36
Extrication • Transpose	37
Adventurous • Enfold Me	38
Resplendent • Accentuate	39
Wonder Full • Sleigh Anyway	40

Happy New Peers • Traverse	41
Equipoise • F.O.E	42
Encumbrance • Decidedly	43
Garden Of The Galaxy • Border Control	44
Lunacy Virtuoso • Jammy Remix	45
Unique Recipe • Perennial	46
Resonant Love • Fancy That	47
Wait For It • Deluge Cometh	48
The Spoils Of War • Casual Causality	49
Fright Or Flight? • Prioritise	50
The Search • Just A Drop	51
Use Your Flipping Head	52
Schooled • Spruce Up	53
Congenial Connection • Get Together	54
Horizon • Uplifted	55
Pep Talk • Database	56
Double Standards • Limited Viability	57
2 Minus 3 • Feet And Funds	58
Doodle-Do • Rudimentary	59

Acquainted • Assess	60
Vent • Tempered	61
Belligerent • Shallow Water	62
Astray • Cloaked	63
Better Help • Blue Feels	64
Shuffle? • Revolving	65
Temperate • Fractured Fractals	66
Upon Reflection • Definitive	67
Thirst For Life • Awash With Beatitude	68
Hilarious • Ta Or Ta-ta!	69
Submerged • Perpetual Illusions	70
Good Knight • Redemption	71
Wash A Shame • Hollow Days	72
Trust • Absolution	73
Overdue • It Costs Nowt	74
Numb The Pain • Whoever Brexit, Buys It	75
Err, Maze Insights • Q And A	76
Picture This • Intimate	77
Torn • Silver	78

Fly Enough To Care	79
Surfs Up • Try, Try, Try	80
Steal Away • Not No News	81
My-All-Stones • Never?	82
Here • Connected	83
Pebble • Deserving	84
Namaste • Beach Bliss	85
Snap Happy • Generosity	86
Puzzled • Endurance	87
Their Purpose	88
About The Author	90
Before You Go...	92

Something Different

Hello, and welcome to the Inspiration Express, tickets please? Thank you. Right, let's get moving shall we...

After two decades of writing mostly full-length poetry, I decided to embrace writing poems that are shorter in length. Some fall under the category of micro-poetry, while other slightly larger pieces would probably be better termed as short poems, the technique of penning poems that are shorter sounds a lot easier than it is, as you have to convey a vivid idea; provide a gripping emotional journey; or deliver a story and a twist, within a small creative space.

Even though I'm a seasoned poet, I find shorter poetry much more challenging to write than regular poems, but they are usually way more satisfying too, as they need to remain concise, but still be impassioned pieces, filled with creativity, insight, and have a deep impact on the reader. I think that these resulting poems of mine, deliver what they set out to and more, but don't take my word for it, have a flick through soon and see for yourself.

So, what is the reasoning behind this book, besides displaying my penmanship and my newfound approach? Well, ultimately, it exists to give you a sneak peek into my unique mind; to feel the warmth of my heart; to allow us both to explore our thoughts and emotions, without feeling judged and alienated; but also to encourage you to smile;

cry if you need to; laugh; become more confident; find your calling; love yourself and others much more; fully embrace your passion; be entertained; to give you something worth pausing and thinking about; and much more.

Now, that is quite a list, right? But I'm confident that this book will deliver, and that you'll come back to these poetic gems time and time again, showing them to friends and loved ones; remembering some of them at relevant points throughout your life; that they'll massively inspire you to go out and grab the life that you want with both hands; and to want to do your bit in making this World a better place.

How many poetry books can you think of, that have such huge aspirations, and strive to give their readers so much? That's why this is something different, it aims to be part of the evolution of poetry, as it's a book of poems that will move you, inspire you, and help you realise you are not alone, instead, we're more alike and interconnected than we realise, and we are all meant for bigger and better things.

So, without further ado, let's embark on the journey of a lifetime!

"Crazy Belief"

Everybody for miles around,
Would point at, tease and laugh at the clown,
Nobody else supported his dream,
They thought he was crazy, and wouldn't believe.

Knowing that the seed inside deserved saving,
Even in this harsh climate, he never gave in,
From the strength, belief and dedication he's shown,
In the desert a prosperous flower has grown.

"Captive-elated"

You've ensnared me, I'm unable to move,
Mesmerised by your beauty, frozen in awe,
I won't even make an effort to break loose,
You're my Stockholm captor, now and ever more.

"No Laughing Matter"

The brutal hyenas laughed at their victim,
Celebrating another successful heist,
Ran off with the spoils and tucked right in,
But to one of the gang, it didn't feel right.

He could no longer mockingly laugh out loud,
Steal for a living, or prey on the weak,
The moment he decided to turn things around,
The World was unlocked, and it lay at his feet.

"Dreams"

It often begins with wishful desire,
Imagining things that we want to achieve,
Time flows and we begin stoking the fire,
Our passion grows strong as we start to believe.

Although, expectations may be misguided,
With new situations, what should we expect,
Keep working at it, and please don't be blinded,
You'll realise your dreams, if you give it your best.

"Within"

Inhalation, now you're inside me,
Spreading throughout, making me lively,
Infusing my cells with enthusiasm,
An ethereal presence, cue ectoplasm.

You remain with me, as I exhale,
We are bonded, connected, your presence prevails,
You fill me with passion and keep me driven.
You're the fuel I thrive on, you're my oxygen.

"Serendipity"

A new adventure is a wonderful thing,
The fresh insight and memories it brings,
Opportunities unravel, your spirit can sing,
A new adventure is a wonderful thing.

Learning something is treasure indeed,
Mistakes or keen study, both will sow seeds,
The riches that bloom, can help you succeed,
Learning something is treasure indeed.

"Dauntless"

Bravery shown above and beyond,
The call of duty or a symbolic bond,
No ego involved, no hidden agenda,
Helping, but not because it'll be remembered.

Just a representation of the finest of traits,
We can display, as the endangered await,
As a job, for your family, a stranger or cat,
There's beauty in an unselfish, heroic act.

"Guilty"

Guilty pleasures weigh upon my mind,
Things I shouldn't like, although I do,
I'm told to have indulgences is fine,
But I guess some adult's choices are taboo.

It's very out of character for sure,
I can't explain the hold it has on me,
However much I have, I still want more,
Lego, will you ever let me be?!

"Onwards"

Into the void, we keep forging on,
Unsure what we'll find, wanting to belong,
Searching for our place in the grandest of schemes,
Desperate to fulfil our hopes and our dreams.

"Wonderment"

A Billion Trillion dots, glowing bright in the sky,
I can't fathom their reach, however much I try,
Each one is larger than this ball of rock I call home,
In true wonderment, I realise how much is... unknown.

"Wormhole Goal"

If a wormhole appeared, what would you do?
Watch from afar, or try to go through?
Just think what could be on the other side,
It could be a lifeline for all humankind.

"Star Of The Show"

The sight of you's delightful, you light up my World,
With you near me, my smiles full, now give us a twirl,
You've put on a light show, you're flashing for me,
There's nothing quite close, to how much I love thee.

"Space To Swing"

I sit and swing, and swing and sit,
Admiring your beauty, bathed in bliss,
These hypnotic glimmers of time now spent,
Truly must be Heaven sent.

"Moon Gazing"

Being beside you, sharing sublime views,
Is humbling, thrilling, my favourite endeavour,
Serenading the Moon with timeless tunes,
We enchant our spirits and merge them together.

"Hero"

With all the grace of an Olympic skater,
She glides through the crowd, nothing can faze her,
Elegance beyond measure, and a heart so pure,
She's an inspiration to mankind, for sure.

"Flow"

You engulf me, caressing my every inch,
You're strong, beautiful, so hard to resist,
If hot, you're excitable, if cool, you're a stiff,
My magical, mysterious, wet little gift.

"Hole Heartedly"

There's a huge hole, where my heart once was,
A colossal space, like peering above,
My chest is caving from its vacuous force,
The only remedy... the return of your love.

"Bituminous"

Winding through darkness,
Lights on the blink,
Travelling at speed,
To find light, I think,
The fear of the shadows,
The thrill of the chase,
I hope that I make it,
To see brighter days.

"Soul-Do-Yours"

Attention! given,
Awaiting orders,
Spiritually driven,
Intentions... flawless,
But who's in command here?
I won't be at ease,
'Til war's reprimanded,
Thus, my soul... will find peace.

"Decisively Foggy"

When the fog comes, be on your guard,
You'll be blind-sided, if you don't focus hard,
Don't idly wait, be smart with your time,
Make every step count, seek out the sunrise!

"Love Locked"

"Keep it locked away!" he heard them say,
"Don't let it be picked, keep the burglars at bay,
Protect your prized treasure, with all of your might,
'Til your soulmate appears, and the moment is right!"

"Know Regrets"

The pain washes over me, consuming me, owning me,
Unable to breathe, I panic and gasp,
My life force deserts me, while schooling me, showing me,
What regrets I will have, if this breath is my... last.

"Pivotal Pursuit"

Find your calling and pursue it,
Whenever you can, enjoy it, do it,
Follow the whispers, own your path,
Be uniquely you, that's all I ask!

"Boldly Go"

How do you leave your imprint, when the path is tough?
Well, treading in paint first, makes your route lighten up,
Steps taken on your journey, determine where you reside,
Remain still and be run over, or pursue your favoured life.

"Upwards"

Defying gravity and supposed insurmountable force,
They left the ground, simply with the power of thought,
"The sky's the limit", was swiftly bellowed by all,
Yet they pierced through the clouds and continued to soar.

"Magic's Cost"

As I float above the hills,
My wish has now come true,
But the thing that made my dreams become real,
Is now shedding its essence in tune.

"Drops 'n' Ducks"

Your opinions clung to me, forming a mask,
My mood and decisions seemed to ripple from you,
But today your words are repelled on contact,
Like water off a duck's back, our connection is through.

"Pack"

You went out alone in bad weather,
Now you're finding it hard to get back,
Heed this, we all eat much better,
When disciplined, and we move as a pack.

"Hopeful"

You're the closest thing to me,

Yet we now feel quite distant,

I see you every day,

But I'm now mostly reminiscent,

Is our magnetism really behind us?

Are the positives slowly transforming into a minus?

I hope we return to our beautiful waltz soon,

In hopeful anticipation, your companion, your moon.

"Remember"

I remember our journey,

I remember our plans,

I remember our hurdles,

And holding your hand,

I recall such great memories,

Big trials we've come through,

So please dear, remember,

How much I love you.

"Puppy Love"

She didn't have a Scooby how he felt,
The Lassie who made his Woofing heart melt,
He pressed Paws, to walk her through,
Dya love me now? I Scooby Doo!

"Solid, Dependable"

I'm rough on the surface, smooth to the touch,
Tough on the critics, disputing our love,
Strong for us both, I'll be your support,
I'll keep out the cold, and whatever comes forth.

"Enlighten-meant"

Beauty emanates from you, amidst darkness,
Untainted by shadows surrounding your being,
The light from your heart, your smile and our lips,
Strengthens our resolve, and keep us believing.

"Love-aluate"

No equation gets to the root of my love,
Representing its power, its impact or mass,
There are no ends or angles, no containing this stuff,
All decay is reversed, as this love's built to last.

"My Sunshine"

Your radiance nourishes me to my roots,
Energising me, helping me grow strong,
When we're together, the goodness shines through,
My cells glow, to show exactly where you belong.

"Chosen"

A blessing to all those privileged to behold her,
Her beauty multiplies as she grows older,
A jewel so rare, she holds mythical stature,
If chosen, you're awarded a lifetime of rapture.

"Quiver"

The sight of you makes my heart
skip, dance and sing,
It flutters with the fervour
of a hummingbird's wings.

"Together"

This eternal bond, built on love unconditional,
Heaven watches the beautiful, sacred vow ritual,
The supreme union of two souls has begun,
Together, every challenge shall be overcome.

"Lively"

Everyone is flying towards the sunset,
Although we'll arrive at our own unique times,
Be deserving of all the great moments you get,
Whatever your age, live the fullest of lives.

"Stop Stopping"

Do not enter, do not pass,
Do not wonder, do not ask,
Do not seek, and do not find,
Yet the brave explorer never resigned.

"Leap"

Don't live with fear, or make friends with sleep,
Have faith in yourself, and take the leap,
It's a proven fact that when you believe,
There's no limit to what you can achieve.

"Determined"

Eyes on the prize, courage on tap,
Stalking my prey, unleashing my wrath,
I know what I want, I'll get the job done,
Exuding prowess, 'til the battle is won.

"Heart-istry"

Cue the canvas, and the paint,
Use the paintbrush, with no restraint,
Paint your heart out, make it count,
The love you put in, is what you'll get out.

"Cirque Du So-Feel"

I dream of the Circus, the magic it brings,
The lions, the elephants, the fiery rings,
The trapeze, trampolines, clever monkeys and clowns,
The World is much brighter, with the Circus in Town.

"Cogitate"

Clockwork android, flesh and steel,
Zero, half or totally real?
Born or made? Inert or alive?
Given a chance... or forced to survive?

"Clocked"

Your HANDS are all over me, in a visual display,
You KEEP me, yet treat me like a sign of decay,
You know WHEN you are with me, any (ME) of the day,
I FRAME all your memories, to RECALL as you may.
I PASS by, you don't see me, only my effects,
I can be an OPPORTUNITY, or a (ME) you regret,
Hopes, fears and decisions, on me you PROJECT,
If you gain MORE of me, usually, you feel blessed.

"Innocence"

The cutest of smiles, the purest of souls,
The blissful ignorance, that you'll one day grow old,
Living in the moment, with a curious mind,
If only we kept the innocence, of a small child.

"Fruitful"

May your journey be fruitful,
May you find what you wish to,
May your lessons be truthful,
Relieve and replenish you.

"Thank You"

My guardian, highlighting the dangers ahead,
Putting my care first, making it easier to cope,
Keeping me more relaxed, than being at home in bed,
The antidote to darkness, my beacon of hope.

"Secure"

Stand fast, look sharp, be bold, act smart,
Hold tight, for sure, got you, secured.

"Ten Out Of Tennis"

LOVE shown by the crowd, while the UMPIRE controls,
The blend of PLAYERS makes for a flavoursome DEUCE,
No animals, but being the G.O.A.T. is the goal,
SERVING SLICES of perfection, like LOBster en croute.
COURT in action, by cameras, watched with a HAWKEYE,
The CHALLENGE is set, they are IN it to win this,
A coveted trophy, and a large NET cash prize,
Immortalised as a CHAMPION after victory's kiss.

"Bwaver-wee"

The young explorer mustered his courage,
And began his spooky adventure,
Due to being recently watered and nourished,
Such a frightful task he had to enter.

He roamed in the dark, battling fear,
"I can do this", he said and believed,
When the cold throne, he'd longed for appeared,
In more ways than one, he was relieved.

"Resonance"

I breathe in deeply, my lips unfurl,
My lungs chase out the gases within,
Time to reach out to the ears of the World,
My throat pulsates, and the noises begin.

My tongue forms words from primitive sounds,
Rolling off the tip, they travel at speed,
To the ears and hearts of those around,
And hopefully give them the fuel that they need.

"Avenged"

The pain I feel, is immeasurable,
At my Sensei's untimely demise,
The culprit has fled, there's a price on his head,
There is nothing else left to decide.

I shall hunt down this retched assassin,
Not for fame or the handsome reward,
Now my Master is gone, I won't truly belong,
'Til our honour has forthwith been restored.

"Game On"

Switched on, we are ready to pursue the exciting,
Minutes pass, the TV screen says LOADING,
Cue the intro, the blocky graphics and writing,
START appears, time for battling and boasting.

Our choices are finalised, the settings configured,
The challenge begins, it's about to get heated,
Laughter, smiles and great memories delivered,
Old school games night, mission completed.

"Rewardzzz"

It's been a long, hard graft,
My body's relieved it's done,
These muscles are feeling the burn,
Their recovery has begun.

I've a huge sense of achievement,
As expectations were steep,
Now I've exceeded my target,
I've earned a bear-sized sleep.

"Steep Odds"

The wily goat sat with a troubled mind,
Dwelling on needs of a nutritional kind,
Sodium ingestion was his requisite,
Without it, the reaper would pay him a visit.

It lay at the top of a very steep dam,
He began to climb, it was his only chance,
The risky feat worked, he dined on his prize,
Not the first time a goat used its head to survive.

"Beyond"

This is not something that I'd usually even try,
It's unnerving working outside of the norm,
I lack know-how, on which I could rely,
I have reservations, qualms, anxiety storms.

No one to hold my hand and walk me through,
My comfort zone is leagues away from here,
I feel exposed, bare, but resolute,
New methods hold potency, beyond the fear.

"Useful"

There's a lot hinging on this, but not in the way you think,
The hinges contain tools, to assist in doing things,
Assembly, survival, parties, exploring,
So many situations where having it is rewarding.

It's compact, strong, sturdy, yet light,
A smart person keeps one close at all times,
One of the things I try to do daily in life,
Is be useful and resilient, like a Swiss Army Knife.

"Aq-we-us"

Clouds of you form right over my head,
The sweet, hot vapour in here is intense,
I knew I loved dew from the moment we met,
Your rare properties capture my every sense.

You refresh, you renew, you're the vessel of life,
Soaking me more than a swim in the sea,
More entwined than merely Husband and Wife,
Drench me with your love Baby, moisturise me.

"Swimathon"

You've been doing lengths inside my mind,
Dwelling in my pool, more than Olympic Swimmers,
Awake, asleep, it matters not, you splash about inside,
I revel in having you in my brain, while you shimmer.

No floats, nothing to restrict your submersion,
Just strokes and styles... breast, back, and butterfly,
Not in it for a medal, just an athlete's perversion,
Freestyle, do what you want while your here, don't be shy.

"Titillated"

Mouth salivating,
Pupils dilating,
Anticipating,
Excited and waiting.

Such a big deal,
I can't conceal,
The way that I feel,
For my favourite meal.

"Combust"

It lurked inside me,
Set things alight,
Slowly grew stronger,
Then burned you alive.

Shone bright, then gently,
Brought you back to life,
My tempestuous, life-giving,
Smouldering fire.

"Firewalker"

Make way, make way, here comes the hot stepper,
Literally, as I walk on hot coals,
For your feet, it's harsher than arctic weather,
But the focus it takes, is so good for your soul.

There's no room for fear, just courage throughout,
If you believe in yourself and channel your chi,
You too can do amazing things, no doubt,
Find out for yourself, don't just take it from me.

"Pow Wow"

The ancient call has now been made,
The elders and tribe members assemble,
Detailed preparations have taken us days,
Timeless rituals performed, as sacred as temples.

Indigenous rites, in ceremonial dress,
You can feel the presence of our ancestors,
We chant, feast and dance, as spirits connect,
Paying tribute to how much this World has blessed us.

"Paradox"

Thinking about mysteries, wonders, possibilities,
I'm enlightened, puzzled, alone, loved, cuddled,
Hearing the seductive whispers of our bountiful Universe,
Feeling both divine and insignificant at the same time.

"Ruffled"

Owl wondered angrily, "hoo in their right mind,
Would want to trick someone hoos trusting and kind?
Owls have a reputation for being very wise,
Yet they make me look stupid, with their twisted lies."

"Why am I so gullible? It's not a natural trait,
For an owl to have, even in this day and age,
They tease me, hurt me, make fun of my pain,
I wish they'd accept hoo I am, and treat me the same!"

"No I In"

Everybody knows their role,
We all have our part to play,
In unison, we advance our goal,
No slacking here, we seize the day.

Our links are strong, no weakness found,
A slick operation, a well oiled machine,
The competition's left for dust on the ground,
When we protect each other and work as a team.

"Deep"

An alien place, shrouded in mystery,
So dark, distant and extremely peculiar,
Housing pressure that would be deadly to me,
Without special equipment, to keep me or you here.

Yet life does flourish in this hostile terrain,
Hidden wonders, that we can barely perceive,
Fascinating features, that I just can't explain,
Like bioluminescence in the deep blue sea.

"Poison"

What's your poison?
Pray, do tell,
Feels like Heaven...
Forged in Hell?

Guilty pleasure?
Tempered vice?
Furtive treasure?
Naughty? Nice?

"Internalise"

Scratching my head,
Feeling confused,
Rigged to explode,
Need to defuse.

Ignore the external,
Focus within,
Locate the pain,
Let the healing begin.

"Alarming"

Waking up flustered,
Feelings of panic,
How could this happen?
I don't understand it!

My plans are ruined,
I'm stuck in a rut,
Why on earth
didn't I get woken up!

"Philanthropy"

A room full of creative minds,
Stalls and gifts, wondrous kinds,
All containing a piece of the sculptor's soul,
A devotion of love, their ultimate goal.

People actively showing support,
All there to raise funds for a noble cause,
A gathering, a chance to buy and sell things,
Plus a charity replenished, everyone wins!

"Hissstory"

Snake-like tactics, slippery moves,
Used by others, felt by you,
Shedding their skin, twisting the truth,
Slithering silently, leaving no clues.

A cold blooded killer, stalking their prey,
Crushing our life force, so we suffocate,
Or fangs inject venom, which eliminates,
Beware of the serpent, or see your last day.

"Would They?"

If only they knew,
This hurt I embody,
Would they empathise?
And would they feel sorry?

Would my good intentions,
Then be understood?
I feel they would not,
But hope that they would.

"Farewell"

Emotions erupting, tearful eyes,
Big mournful hugs, while saying goodbye,
Holding on tight, no desire to let go,
Hearts on sleeves, feelings on show.

Bye-bye for a season, or maybe for good,
I'll still hold you dear, like my own flesh and blood,
You've made my life brighter, and filled it with joy,
Your absence, will leave my heart with a void.

"Lonely Hollow"

My heart is swiftly faltering,
As I ingress into digression,
This stomach's caustically churning,
While I fall into a solitary dimension.

Lurking shadows envelop my being,
The cold encroaches, bitterness follows,
In need of help, I'm begging, pleading,
Will someone please save me, from Lonely Hollow?!

"Restitution"

Visceral vices,
Instincts at work,
Intellect bypassed,
Common sense swerved.

Toxins, we digest,
Goodness rebuked,
How can well-being,
Resume, restitute?

"Catalyst"

If my life had been less eventful,
Would I still strive to reach my full potential?
Without my past hardships, turmoil and stress,
Would I still find the fuel to rise to the test?

I've come a long way, from where I began,
All I've endured, helps me understand,
The struggles of others, and aide their repair,
Pain turns into a catalyst, do not despair.

"Extrication"

Divine intentions,
Defying dimensions,
Reclining in Heaven,
But still somehow here.

Sight misrepresented,
Guised as intended,
Misaligned, yet mended,
No more prisons of fear.

"Transpose"

Return to maker, or spares and repairs,
A reckless user, caught my mind unawares.
Return to maker, unwanted gift,
The giver didn't study my explicit wish list.

Return to maker, too complex for them all,
Does not compute, manufacturer recall.
Return to maker, they have no respect,
Their software's corrupted, factory reset.

"Adventurous"

We're off on a quest, but don't know where to,
The destination is wherever we choose,
No need for protection, coats or shoes,
Whatever the weather, there'll be plenty to do.

An indoor adventure, the best of its kind,
Diving into the breach, to see what we find,
The prospects on offer, are simply sublime,
When we delve inside, the depths of our minds.

"Enfold Me"

Heads up, I'm a hugger, through and through,
You'll get a good squeeze, if you like hugs too,
Don't get me wrong, I'm not one to impose,
You'll only get one, if it's mutually chose.

If you prefer waves, that's what you'll receive,
Handshakes, I'll connect at the end of your sleeve,
But when a warm snuggle, is more your thing,
This runway's clear, go ahead, bring it in!

"Resplendent"

Your twinkling eyes,
Shimmering limbs,
Sparkling smile,
And radiant skin,

Bright mind,
Sunny disposition,
Inside you,
And outside... you glisten!

"Accentuate"

Although our devotion is premeditated,
It ebbs and flows freely, unregulated,
No clauses on how it should be demonstrated,
The result, our affection is accentuated.

We highlight the beauty, natural and pure,
Elevating each other, we can't see the floor,
Always a thrill, never a bore,
We surrender, OMNIA VINCIT AMOR.

"Wonder FULL"

Land of wonder, time of joy,
Sprinkles of magic for us to enjoy,
Winter enchantment, mystic beliefs,
An excuse to gormandise festive treats.

Although we acquire, there's a focus on giving,
Downgraded working, prioritised living,
But the best thing about this time, that really rocks,
Is a child shunning toys, mesmerised by a box.

"Sleigh Anyway"

Whispers the red-clothed wordsmith,
Had a very shiny head,
And if you ever saw it,
You'd know that his hair had shed,

Some of the hairy people,
Used to laugh and call him names,
But Whispers, he kept on shining,
'Cos he knew we are all the same!

"Happy New Peers"

We have now entered a new segment in time,
The old one has passed, such heights we climbed!
Some see this switch over as a clean slate,
A chance for new hopes, to start over, be great.

The truth of the matter, it's purely symbolic,
No countdown's needed to have tort demolished,
You are beautiful, and you can be more so in fact,
By not waiting for a "right time" to improve how you act.

"Traverse"

Travelling at the speed of light,
I wonder, what I'd even see?
Could I finally witness the slowing of time,
Would the expanding Universe now be perceived?

Might I then, lose sight of Earth?
Using tachyons, could I go even faster?
Rewinding time, realising my worth,
Becoming The Doctor, rebuffing The Master.

"Equipoise"

I feel like you're winning, a worrying statement,
Trespassing, kicking my lungs to the pavement,
My defences are strong, versus general invasions,
But this attack seems like an elimination.

You must be mutating, to do this much damage,
I've played by the rules, but they're not in your language,
I need to find parity, reclaim my Yang-age,
Your Yin is too dominant, must, restore, balance.

"F.O.E"

Friend or foe?
Constraint or reprieve?
Sentence of no,
Or yes I believe?

Full of emptiness,
Or purpose restored?
Wield your finesse,
Feel Overawed Evermore.

"Encumbrance"

The race has begun,
It'll challenge your mettle,
The fight's no longer hidden,
There's a point to be settled.

Dig deep and continue,
Obstacles, meet with force,
You have strength within you,
Spank the assault course.

"Decidedly"

Difficult choices lay in wait,
Is life prewritten, a product of fate?
I don't think so, I control my own life,
Milestones are aligned, based on what I decide.

Emotions cloud judgement, thus logic's rewritten,
Would my future self, praise my indecision?
Here's a helpful exercise I recommend...
What advice would you give, if your life was your friend's?

"Garden Of The Galaxy"

I'm not Groot, but I am rooted,
Deeply planted, firmly footed,
Stable and nourished, certain of this,
The soil that I occupy's nutrient rich.

As a struggling seed, I yearned to survive,
Sought out better pastures, started to thrive,
To those wanting blossoms to sprout from within,
Be mindful of the turf you embed yourself in.

"Border Control"

You are one country, I am another,
If you invade, my sovereignty suffers,
I'm able to grant you access inside,
But for toxic diplomats... visa denied.

I'd like nothing more than to trade with your nation,
Although, my first focus is self preservation,
When you're considerate, with morals that glow,
I'll open my borders, and friendship can flow.

"Lunacy Virtuoso"

I'm a bit loopy, misunderstood, weird,
Yet this brand of cuckoo, is seldom revered,
If I'd been alive in centuries past,
The powers that be, would section my ass.

My eccentric views are offensive to some,
Those wanting to keep us in turmoil and dumb,
So the search continues, in the hope that I'll find,
More wonderful, passionate, peculiar minds.

"Jammy Remix"

The Mad Hatter was tired of tea and cake,
He concluded his party required an update,
Uncle Winston's cookbook was an interesting read,
"A Caribbean twist, could be just what we need!"

March Hare found ingredients, Dormouse assisted,
Alice joined the others at work in the Kitchen,
Bun an' cheese, saltfish fritters, they made plenty to munch,
Then they merrily feasted and sipped Guinness Punch.

"Unique Recipe"

This World of ours, has billions of dishes,
Yet total transformation are their most common wishes,
A disservice to how yummy, they already are,
Loving your essence, leads to Michelin Stars.

The smallest of tweaks, should be all that's desired,
Just to celebrate your beautiful mystique and style,
You're way more delicious than you give credit for,
Your unique flavour's precious, can we please have some more?

"Perennial"

Carefully bolted tight, greased and covered,
Our love is secure, not flaunted or smothered,
It's not in a pageant, nor seeking a prize,
The title "World's Greatest", is felt, not implied.

I pray that we never become big-headed,
Take this bond for granted, or get our bolts threaded,
Future-focused, we don't dwell on the past,
Encased in titanium, strong, built to last.

"Resonant Love"

The Wedding Singer stepped up to the mic,
A tender inflection came out of his pipes,
The crowd stood amazed by this wondrous sound,
He sang love songs, some his own, some renowned.

To a magical world, he transported them all,
The crowd were spellbound and deeply enthralled,
After five encores, his crooning subdued,
As he left, you could still feel the love in the room.

"Fancy That"

Magnetism that pulls you in on sight,
The attraction just happens, it can't be denied,
Strong yearnings erupt, from way deep inside,
You must keep your cool, as a matter of pride.

As excited as a puppy, with new toy in tow,
Heartbeat racing, you're about to explode,
Buttons fondled, cue continuous flow,
Of the new season of your favourite show!

"Wait For It"

This thing's filled with uncertainty,
Stretching far into the distance,
Steadily stealing my time from me,
Success requires patience and persistence.

I have a goal, that I aim to complete,
Although I do wonder, what am I doing!?
It's rewarding, but generally bitter sweet,
A typical experience in the art of queueing.

"Deluge Cometh"

What is that, sprawled across my bed?!
I see it, and blood rushes straight to my head,
My jaw hits the floor, I cannot believe,
The audacity, look at the bare faced cheek!

Did you plan this, or did it just happen this way?
My eye glimpses wetness, resembling a wave,
Overcome, I come over and firmly request,
"Don't leave wet towels, in the place where I rest!"

"The Spoils Of War"

One might think, that might is mighty important,
When seeking the approach, to best procure treasure,
One side lays siege, while the other lies dormant,
Is overcome and suffers defeats beyond measure.

One feels victorious, the other defeated,
Though both are cheated, in this plunderous art,
Prolonging this charade, both will be depleted,
'Til the mind, finally makes peace with the heart.

"Casual Causality"

The cause, the effect,
The force of neglect,
Reflective responses,
To the heart that's bereft.

Trivial aberration,
Captive frustrations,
Don't ignore the monsters,
Care for the patience.

"Fright Or Flight?"

Two beady eyes, gazing profusely,
The World passes by, while I'm being reclusive,
Passing up opportunities, a slave to the bells,
The alarms keep on sounding, so I stay in my shell.

My heart wants to soar, but it's not happening,
Confined in a shell, you can't flap your wings,
I need to break free, but I'd then be exposed,
If I don't go, it'll hamper my life and my growth.

"Prioritise"

What's best for me? Is my best before me?
Pain - best before: March 2016,
Long overdue, overdue some release,
More sorrow ensues, 'til I find some relief!

I've got to let go of the pain and the grief;
The baggage; distractions... all stuck on repeat,
It's time to refocus, focus on me,
Self love and respect are top priority.

"The Search"

I look up and down, to the left and the right,
Searching for something, just out of sight,
Calling out to me, whispering truths,
But as hard as I hunt, it remains out of view.

I use a telescope, to extend my focus,
The further I scan, the more it seems hopeless,
Maybe I've failed! It must have escaped!
I blink and it's staring me right in the face.

"Just A Drop"

A drop in the ocean, lost its way,
Evaporated, then, in the sky it did stay,
Met others who could relate to its dilemma,
They united and formed big rain clouds together.

To onlookers, the outlook may have looked bleak,
Grey clouds, close to bursting, an emotional feat,
They returned to the sea, a rainbow appeared,
See, a minuscule droplet, can indeed be revered!

"Use Your Flipping Head"

Every story, every coin,
The two sides remain, until destroyed,
But the story's parts, may overlap,
The spun coin, on its edge may land.

Both can be flipped, to change their view,
One's solid, the other presents the truth...
In varied degrees, odd semblant reflections,
Coins can mask truth, change people's perceptions...

If enough are combined, to sway their belief,
True words can slay demons, coins are a sheath,
Stick to your truth, do not be swayed,
Your story's important,
please don't be dismayed.

"Schooled"

There's truly no shame in stumbling or falling,
Life can be hard, it can strike without warning,
Ruining best laid plans, stifling your progress,
Testing your mettle, in a sink or swim process.

Experience is the greatest teacher around,
When you get up, that's where strength is found,
The challenges we face are a mental boot camp,
The quicker you learn, the swifter you advance.

"Spruce Up"

Declutter your soul,
On junk, go to Town,
Ascension's the goal,
But what's holding you down?

Don't hoard bulky baggage,
It's serving no use,
Just tend to the damage,
Then pursue your truth.

"Congenial Connection"

Are you even remotely in tune with me?
Do your vibes complement my deep frequency?
Are your batteries low? Can you influence change?
Are there technical problems that you can't contain?

Do you still promote love, when your transmitter Hertz?
Can you be "one-for-all" while displaying self worth?
Harmony is the goal, unity resonates,
When linked positively, we will all elevate.

"Get Together"

Plans have been made, supplies acquired,
No open-door policy, invite required,
It's been quite a while, since we all converged,
Life's demands, kept our gathering deferred.

But now we're together, in boundless hysterics,
The fun, games and laughter, we'll never forget it,
Such a blessing it is, sharing moments like these,
Refreshing us, just like a cool summer breeze.

"Horizon"

The vessel's horn bellows, the anchor's retrieved,
The journey begins on the vast open seas,
Meanwhile on the harbour, loved ones are gathered,
As the ship pulls away, their hearts are in tatters.

It feels like desertion, but it must be this way,
We've so much to do, otherwise we would stay,
The horizon engulfs the craft's blurry image,
Our story's on pause, but God willing, not finished.

"Uplifted"

The gentlest of breezes, moves me profoundly,
Serenading my substance, glad to have found me,
I feel myself rising, I'm as light as a feather,
I could honestly stay this way, floating forever.

Clarity's crystal in this birds-eye view,
My insight's restored, then balance ensues,
I return to the ground, descending with whimsy,
To take all my friends, on a magic flight with me.

"Pep Talk"

"It's about to get heated inside of my cheeks!"
Said the Cayenne, Serrano and Haberno freak,
"My tongue will dance, while Facing Heaven,
No Dragon's Breath, but staunch Scoville ascension."

"Scotch Bonnet, Bird's Eye, and the venerable Ghost,
It's hard to decide which one I love most,
The feverous flavours, the toilet you tether...
The gift and the curse of a spirited pepper."

"Database"

This service is free, we just need your details,
We may pass this on to our partners... discreet fail,
Your personal information is the new currency,
When used, get bombarded with things you don't need!

Hackers might acquire it, and begin cunning games,
With the ultimate goal, of getting credit in your name,
You don't want a debt collector, barging through your door,
Be careful what you give out, seek advice if unsure!

"Double Standards"

Words are dried up, I'm at a loss,
To describe how you cheated me, matt is not gloss,
You promised me one thing, delivered another,
An inferior substitute, you mother sufferer.

You brushed off my efforts to address the matter,
You PayPals hush money, ensuring disaster,
My claim is declined on the frailest of posits,
Protection my arse, they have you in their pocket!

"Limited Viability"

A product is conceived in the depths of a mind,
A factory calibrated to build the design,
The resources needed, acquired by the tonne,
The workforce has arrived, and production's begun.

These items fill warehouses, shops and our homes,
Tiny faults ensue, the products... disowned,
Things don't last any more, in this throw-away culture,
But resources are finite, so what of our future?!

"2 Minus 3"

"Look what I brought, Look what I did!"
Great, there goes a few hundred quid!
"I got us these things (that we really don't need),
Oh, we're overdrawn!" ...cue charges and fees.

"Should we get those?" "No, we don't need them now",
"Tadaah! I've purchased what we spoke about!"
"Is this our joint account, or your spending fund?
You're spending my patience, my smile is undone."

"Feet And Funds"

The products we use, and the things that we buy,
Imprint this World with the values inside,
If we support firms that damage the planet,
We can't claim to care, by any means, damn it!

The impact of livestock for human consumption,
Our throwaway culture, and wasteful production,
Earth can't take much more, we're treated like fools,
But our choices and money are powerful tools.

"Doodle-Do"

When the Rooster calls, what's your response?
Do you leap out of bed, and get to it at once,
With a huge smile, greeting the new day head on,
Or become bitter, frustrated or nonchalant?

Not everyone hears the Rooster's loud beckon,
Someone's time is up, with each passing second,
Be fuelled by your blessings, inspired by your lessons,
That's my take on things, but what do YOU reckon?

"Rudimentary"

There's so much I don't know, will you please explain?
Too embarrassed to ask, and I know I'm a pain,
Hormones going loopy, refurb's in my brain,
I'm going through changes, again and again.

Such a confusing time, more complex than it seems,
This makes me blunt, I don't mean to be mean,
I've got so many doubts plaguing my self-esteem,
The testing reality of being a Teen.

"Acquainted"

I've noticed, my alias neglects formality,
You don't know my name, only my personality,
Sure, you can call me Friend, or Following Whispers,
But, if you're wondering, my real name is Clinton.

I live in the UK, with my Wife and four kids,
I'm a self-professed Geek, and a sucker for a quiz,
I made music, before poetry claimed my heart,
I don't think my pen and I, will ever part.

"Assess"

Monitor entity, study identity,
Findings, bring plenty please,
If friendly, meant for me,
Tentatively, cue next entry...

Mode selected, thoughts detected,
Data collected, host receptive,
Introspective, core directive,
Don't you mess with, focused settings.

"Vent"

I'm fuming, fuming, totally fuming,
Toxically spewing, venom I'm brewing,
Infectious, protect yourself if you're 'round me,
I mean no harm, but I'm struggling profoundly.

Pent up, suffocating, hazardous smog,
Gassing the environment, like a warthog,
I need to rotate, 180 the hate,
Deep breath, fresh air, ventilate.

"Tempered"

Breathe in, breathe out, count to ten,
"It didn't work!" Then do it again,
Deeper breaths, count more slowly,
Dispel those thoughts deemed unholy.

You'll only be mad at yourself afterwards,
So don't do it, it's really not worth the fuss,
Calm yourself down, don't pull out your hair,
"Phew, I dodged a huge bullet there!"

"Belligerent"

Heated scenarios, heated words,
Heated discussions, nouns and verbs,
Heated temperaments, heated expressions,
Heated results, born of heated intentions.

Hot potato, submerged in hot topics,
Hot tempered folk, defying all logic,
Hot off the press... *"Friends Make Amends"*,
Now that we've cooled off, we're Besties again.

"Shallow Water"

How much water is dangerous?
Some would say, merely a gulp,
When it goes down the wrong way,
It can mess you up, or stop your pulse.

Just because something appears to be small,
Doesn't mean it can't pack a punch,
Respect everything, despite appearances,
Or you'll be the one, being somebody's lunch.

"Astray"

I've no indication of where I now stand,
There are no signs, maps, or warm guiding hands,
No lights or voices, to steer my direction,
I wait in the dark, with my mind for protection.

If I stay put, I'll be this way forever,
I'm scared, but prolonged loneliness is no better,
I'd see more here if I plucked out both my eyes,
No more shall I walk on a path full of lies.

"Cloaked"

Behind the scenes, mysterious things are occurring,
Some for our benefit, but many are disturbing,
Some efforts are helping, elevating humankind,
Other forces are harmful, warping our minds...

Bombarding our bodies, poisoning by design,
Toxins, additives, acidic food, stealthy genocide,
Frequencies distorted, secret scientific perversion,
If we don't reverse these ill effects, life will clearly worsen.

"Better Help"

I must take care of my family and friends,
Oops, I think I overdid it again,
I forgot to eat something, while tending to others,
Now drained, I wish I could hide under the covers.

I've been a huge help, but forgot to drink,
Dehydrated, deflated, unable to think,
I'm little use now my vitality's gone,
I must set myself to Priority One.

"Blue Feels"

Feel better Blue, your demeanour is impish,
You ignored the signs, now the fire won't extinguish,
You've favoured short gains, causing long-term losses,
It's high time you demonstrated who the Boss is.

Your body is warning you something is wrong,
Harnessing pure nature is how you grow strong,
Eat alkaline; hydrate; detoxify... proof,
I'm glad you've begun to feel better Blue.

"Shuffle?"

We are all dealt cards, some we wish we never had,
It's all part of the balance of the Universal pack,
We may swap out a card, hoping for better wealth,
But, should also appreciate the hand we've been dealt.

Seemingly weak cards, can end up being game changers,
You can fold, but are you doing yourself any favours?
We've no way of knowing, exactly what's coming next,
Be certain of your choice, before reshuffling the deck.

"Revolving"

I can't quite recall, when I stepped in,
Sensing my presence, it started to spin,
The speed startled me, almost mowing me down,
Caught up in the chase, I kept going around.

Four options: two exits; keep circling; get splattered;
I secured my freedom, realising what matters,
No longer in limbo, I'm back on my way,
But this big ball I'm stuck on, I'm yet to escape.

"Temperate"

At times we'll face attacks on our person,
Character and morals, of this I'm certain,
Often, we fear what we don't understand,
No awareness is sought, we just reprimand.

But if someone is doing wrong in your eyes,
Find the root motivation, that's hidden behind,
You can still love someone, when you don't like them,
Find their humanity, then help to revive them.

"Fractured Fractals"

Tiny fragments, from that once complete,
Spanning forever, as the pattern repeats,
Swirls of emotions, with quantum infusion,
Entangled in something both real and illusion.

The deeper you delve, the more truths unfold,
From macro to micro, shell to the soul,
Intrinsic resonance, information dispatch,
Inside lies the code to the way we react.

"Upon Reflection"

Reminiscing on times, that now serve as a glimmer,
Rewinding to when life was oh so much simpler,
Reflecting on choices, and the outcomes that followed,
The yearning, the lessons, the ego now swallowed.

Though simpler, life back then was much more hurtful,
But the pain helped to train me, and my inner-circle,
We now stand as guardians, of love; freedom; light;
Every moment's brought greater meaning to my life.

"Definitive"

Life can be brutal, it can knock you about,
Testing your substance, pushing you down,
Some hit the ground and opt to stay put,
Believing the worst, their response is "enough!"

Others face hardships you couldn't imagine,
Bombarded, they still send the bad vibes packing,
The definition of courage, resilience and hope,
These are the souls, that I respect the most.

"Thirst For Life"

First off, you amaze me, you warm my heart,
I could see your warrior spirit, right from the start,
Your strength's inspiring, you put mine to shame,
That's not your intention, your fight's just insane!

Life's dealt you tough cards, that would break other beings,
You're a champion of light, joy, love and warm feelings,
No complaints from you, just smiles and swagger,
Your thirst for life fills us with hope that won't shatter.

"Awash With Beatitude"

I've an affinity with water, it quenches my soul,
Sensing it, makes my spirit feel whole,
Its effects are strengthened in a natural setting,
Lakes, rivers and seas, to me, are a blessing.

I watch its wild dance, it is truly enticing,
Finding life in its flow, which at first, was surprising,
Waves of energy caress me, uplifting my being,
When near water, there's no end to the joy I am feeling.

"Hilarious"

Ear to ear, as wide as can be,
A big happy smile, resonating with glee,
Body convulsing from hilarity,
The roars of laughter, in need of release.

Cheek muscles burning, pleasure and pain,
Back of the head, really feeling the strain,
Fun makes dopamine flow to the brain,
Wondrous moments, long may they remain.

"Ta Or Ta-ta!"

We can sometimes be smug with the life that we have,
Or even detest it, always feeling bad,
Either way, not appreciating what we are blessed with,
Circumstances that billions would kill to be left in.

Yet we have a good moan, engage in long sulks,
Or think we're invincible, just like The Hulk,
I'd show that you're thankful, If I were you,
Things could change in a blink, to a perilous doom.

"Submerged"

It's the end, we've faced horrors like you've never seen,
The World that we knew, is a distant memory,
History's been erased, nothing left to believe,
It's just me, my crew, and this grand submarine.

We're thousands of leagues under, sheltered from harm,
It's increasingly difficult to keep the crew calm,
Our dwindling supplies are a cause for alarm,
We need to resurface, before things fall apart.

"Perpetual Illusions"

Enduring images plaguing the mind,
No rest for the wickedness making you blind,
Ceaseless immersion in groundless fallacies,
Shielded from truth, love, light, and reality.

Our senses are fooled, we're made to feel helpless,
The power's entrusted to those who won't help us,
It's time to remove their virtual prison,
By freeing our minds, our souls, and our vision.

"Good Knight"

Laced in chainmail, huge, heavy armour,
Longswords ready to fend off failure,
Valiant deeds conjured in legendary fashion,
No one can question their virtue and passion.

They fend off attackers, and beasts of lore,
Through honourable methods, they even the score,
Defending our realm, they sacrifice freely,
Thanks to their efforts, my family sleep easy.

"Redemption"

Everyone else thought it couldn't be won,
But we believed we could get the job done,
And sometimes that is all that it takes,
Belief in yourself, wisdom from your mistakes.

We achieved what we said we'd do from the start,
Meeting fierce resistance, with the strength of our hearts,
The odds we defied, left onlookers stunned,
But I feel that our best, is still yet to come!

"Wash A Shame"

One thing that really infuriates me,
Are those who don't handwash after they pee,
Men are awful, around half see no problem,
When I see them walk out, I feel I should stop them.

Do they realise the germs they are spreading about,
As they infect doors and things on their way out,
Then they touch people; eat; work with food; hold children;
Until they're hygienic, I'll keep a safe distance.

"Hollow Days"

Excitement intensifies as the moment draws near,
For children, it may well be the best time of the year,
Of course, I refer to the precious Summertime,
Its fond memory potential, is totally sublime.

But if my kids act up again, bang goes the dream,
They'll stare at these walls, with no technology,
If you can't show respect, I'll have my fun indoors,
While you regret your choices, and waste away, bored.

"Trust"

When things don't add up, and your instincts are calling,
You sometimes dig deeper, and find holes in stories,
We made a promise, about the way that we'd act,
But why am I the only one, sticking to our pact?!

I've kept to our arrangement, you didn't feel the need,
You clearly think it's okay going back on what's agreed,
Apparently, your word means squat, where to from here?
Are you going to stay nonchalant, and watch it disappear?

"Absolution"

You may want my forgiveness,
But it comes at a price, see,
I'm not cleaning the slate,
Just because you asked nicely.

You've got your work cut out,
To earn my favour again,
So, when you think you're ready,
I'll be here, in my den.

"Overdue"

As I grow older, I'm increasingly sick of it,
The younger generations are accustomed to privilege,
The World's their oyster, they want for so little,
But the value of something's the hardest of riddles.

They haven't a clue, they've been spoilt with excess,
Things on tap, to avoid tantrums and unwanted stress,
But the long term cost is that nothing's been earned,
So there'll be no respect, 'til this lesson's been learned.

"It Costs Nowt"

Young ones disrespecting their elders and parents,
Speaking with venom as their default setting,
Conversations are conflict, full of ignorance,
No interest, if it's not about what they're getting.

The result, we drift further and further apart,
Have no common ground, can't see eye to eye,
Warm emotions - off limits, I feel it's time to start,
Ensuring they have warmth, and are always polite.

"Numb The Pain"

Clingfilm my senses, please wrap them up,
Don't let them out, don't let them be touched,
I can't chance feeling, just one more emowsh,
Could tip me into phases of being exposed.

Save me from the fierce pull of this tug of war,
It leaves me with rope burns, overwhelmingly sore,
Come to think of it, my resistance makes the pain,
I need to let go, and become whole again.

"Whoever Brexit, Buys It"

The one who Brexit, will feel the cost,
But have nothing to show, for the money they've lost,
Really, the product was broken before,
The description didn't match, what they had in store.

Unelected peers governing sovereign nations,
Buggered... choose no democracy, or bad relations,
We gave money; gold; now our spirit, they'll rob it,
But in fairness, look at who, we left in charge of it.

Err, Maze Insights"

Are you currently stuck in a worrying maze?
Are you scared of being trapped and wasting away?
Here's a trick, choose a side, put your hand on that wall,
Keep walking forward, and you'll reach your reward.

As long as they don't reconfigure or move,
It'll be alright, you'll find your way through,
The other option's to climb up and move on the top,
With a better perspective, there's no way you'll get lost.

"Q And A"

"Who am I? Where am I? Where is my place?
How did it come to this? What is my fate?
Where do I go from here? Do I belong?
Can I turn it 'round? Why is everything wrong?"

"You are the light that we need in this World,
You're here to claim your space, as your heart unfurls,
Spread love and acceptance, then you'll find your home,
It'll improve, this is just a bump in your road."

"Picture This"

The most exquisite of paintings,
Drew an unparalleled crowd,
Nobody had seen such beauty before,
A sight to bring joy and astound.

The absent artist was unknown,
They viewed her work with fresh eyes,
When they were told, that she had no arms,
They were immensely inspired and surprised.

"Intimate"

If Adele sang for 60 people, let's speculate,
Does it make her performance any less great?
Not at all, she's one of the best, that's a fact,
The crowd size won't diminish, her perfected craft.

A super-creative mind self-publishes again,
Using their money and time, to show the life in their pen,
Some of the most amazing artistry, that few will ever read,
I praise your valiant efforts, and inside, my heart bleeds.

"Torn"

You passed away, I miss you so much,
I think of you often, probably more than I should,
As I'm still here breathing, but I'm stuck in a loop,
Missing your presence, and the essence of you.

However, your suffering and pain are no more,
Your spirit is free, you can finally soar,
I must find a way to stop feeling conflicted,
Then smile at our blessings, not live like a nitwit.

"Silver"

Dark clouds approaching, looking quite furious,
Heavily burdened, yet I don't hide, I'm curious,
To find out the source and cause of this storm,
Its reason for being, no matter how raw.

We get chatting, the clouds grew with good intentions,
But external factors made them angry, they mention,
I said, "you're a blessing, look... life, you deliver!
They've got it all wrong man, you're not grey, you're silver!"

"Fly Enough To Care"

I'm a Vegan and care deeply about animal welfare,
But when it comes to pests, I'd rather be elsewhere,
Although, thanks to my love and appreciation of nature,
I did something recently, not seen as normal behaviour.

I made friends with a common house fly in my home,
I house-trained it, to leave certain things alone,
For weeks it sat on my knee, and we watched TV,
Honest, ask my Wife and Kids, if you don't believe me.

My little fly friend taught me a valuable lesson,
Without fear and violence, we find a kinder connection,
I still don't like pests that cause harm physically,
But humans in general, should embrace each other fully.

If I can love a fly, and fly can love me,
And we can co-exist, enjoying each other's company,
Surely, despite our differences, humans can too,
Then we can watch love grow, much quicker than bamboo.

"Surfs Up"

What are the greatest problems in your life?
Describe the struggles that fill you with strife?
What have you tried, which approaches are left?
When you find the right fix, you'll feel much less depressed.

Life's one big lesson, there's so much to learn,
It's amazing how pain can instruct us to surf,
To ride the next wave to the barrel's end,
Your instructor can help you to hang loose, my friend.

"Try, Try, Try"

It won't sit right with me, it's just not working,
All the work I've put in, is it really worth it?
I want the result, but the effort's exhausting,
I'd be glad of a shortcut, even though it's naughty.

I'd like to earn my stripes, but don't think I can,
I've tried and I've tried, now it's sending me mad,
Oops, wait a minute, forget what I stated,
I've done it, I've cracked it, I've finally made it!

"Steal Away"

I listen keenly, the stethoscope's applied,
Turning the dial, trying to learn the mysteries inside,
After patient persistence, I hear what I seek,
Cracking the safe, its secrets are within my reach.

As I scan the contents, there's the strangest of vibes,
Everything I put my hand to, I oddly, recognise,
Oh my days, I've literally been stealing from home,
I found my safe place, learning things I should've known.

"Not No News"

Something inside's not been right for a while,
I have good days and bad, off days and hell,
More toughies than not, I do my best to smile,
But now I'm in the hospital, very unwell.

The results are in, and the news is, well, bad,
They say that it's terminal, the timer's been set,
While I still have life in me though, I will fight back,
It's not over 'til I say it is, so cheer up Pet!

"My-All-Stones"

Steps we take, to complete our goals,
Points we have passed, after gaining control,
Ports we dock in, with our ship-shape vessel,
The way that we glow, after gaining our petals.

Milestones are a great way to measure progress,
But can be too conventional, bringing you stress,
Here's the greatest milestone, to fill you with cheer,
It's a brand new day, and you... are still here!

"Never?"

"Never say never!" (old advice from my Mum),
But what if I say that "I'll never give up!"?
A statement of intent, a promise to self,
An energy, that will be both seen and felt.

"I will honour my ancestors, nourish my soul,
Continue to spread love, focus on my role,
I'll dispel the darkness, fight for what's right,
I won't give up making the most of my life."

"Here"

We've all been tasked with walking this Earth,
But some of us look like we're pushing a hearse,
I see them struggling with monstrous pain,
Their rigid walk shows, they're feeling the strain.

I'll help put your burden, where it belongs,
Once it's in the ground, you'll see it's made you strong,
You've kept battling, for that, you have my respect,
When we're done, you'll have a spring in your step.

"Connected"

I'm here for you, you're here for me,
I've got your back with whatever you need,
The sentiment's mutual, a bond born of love,
A strong, warm connection, simply because.

Your beauty's astounding, it shines from within,
And on its way out, it blesses your skin,
Plus everything else that it then embraces,
In this World's wonders, I see your traces.

"Pebble"

You've had a tough life, been battered by the sea,
Waves wore you down, changed your identity,
No longer resembling, the rock you once were,
A fragment of your former self, you shun your worth.

But the Universe works in mysterious ways,
You're more beautiful, thanks to the hardships you've faced,
You're a smooth, shiny pebble, a gorgeous soul,
A treasure, a keepsake, a pleasure to hold.

"Deserving"

My body's a temple, I'll treat it as such,
When I try to cut corners, the cost is too much,
For each toxic substance I allow through my door,
The results that unfold, will punish me more.

Not respecting the value of my precious body,
Will defeat my good efforts, leaving me sorry,
For my well being, sanctity must be preserved,
My body is sacred, reverence is deserved.

"Namaste"

Eye to eye, soul to soul,
A meeting of minds, uncovering gold,
I see your aura, it complements mine,
Shining so vividly, bright and divine.

As our spirits converge, cosmic poetry's born,
This love and empathy, keeps our hearts warm,
The Universe salutes us for the light we share,
Your presence has blessed me, I know that you care.

"Beach Bliss"

Sand between my toes, yet the waves refresh,
Not only cleansing them, but they wash away stress,
The sights are truly magic, with mesmerising hold,
The sounds and smells are wondrous, uplifting my soul.

One of my favourite places, to dwell upon this earth,
My love's not overstated, I revel in your worth,
I hope we do not ruin you, you have so much to give,
I'm forever grateful to you, for filling me with bliss.

"Snap Happy"

There are so many moments, that I can recall,
That bring immense joy, to my heart and my spirit,
Warm, fuzzy feels, when the image installs,
Precious gems fill me, as memories visit.

I have snapshots of amazing, priceless adventures,
My album's filling quickly, but there's more to see,
When I'm in a nursing home, rocking my dentures,
I'll revel at my wonderful Polaroid Tree.

"Generosity"

There's a limited view of what generous means,
Tied to giving an object, money and things,
But it really means so much more than that,
There need be no transfer of ownership, fact.

Give out hugs, mend wounds, gift a smile,
Care for your neighbour, lend an ear for a while,
Find someone lonely and spend time together,
Any one of these deeds, can change lives for the better.

"Puzzled"

Starting with a muddled and chaotic mess,
I begin to decipher the puzzle I'm set,
Seeing fragments of something with much deeper meaning,
As I connect the pieces, more truth I'm revealing.

I drink in the beauty of the greater design,
As the secrets unfold, they strengthen my mind,
The mystery's solved, understanding's received,
But what if this puzzle, is merely one piece!?

"Endurance"

You had me from the introduction,
Between the lines, I sensed seduction,
Satisfaction promised... will you deliver?
As I study you deeper, my lips, they quiver.

I touch you gently, and thus you respond,
Of this shared journey, I'm overly fond,
You kept your promise, but I yearn for more,
The power of a book made with love, will endure.

"Their Purpose"

These arms were made for giving,
Building, supporting and hugging,
They will not endanger the living,
But will act as a vessel for loving.

This heart was made to celebrate life,
Every intricate piece, honoured in beat,
Pumping affection, encouraging light,
In love with the beauty it feels, and it sees.

This person was made to love their neighbour,
To embrace every single thing in existence,
Strengthen connections, make us all braver,
And speak the truth, as the Universe listens.

About The Author

Hello, I'm Following Whispers, an English poet and author who has been writing poetry for over two decades. I was initially inspired to put pen to paper, after a series of difficult events, that shook me to the core, which left me struggling to make sense of what had happened and why; make sense of the somewhat merciless world around me; my emotions; who I was; and more importantly, who I wanted to become.

I am a self-professed Geek who can get deep sometimes (as I have done for most of this book), but I generally don't take myself too seriously, I just love to have fun, inspire others, plus be inspired by the things and people all around me.

In my early twenties, I realised that beauty could be born out of not only love, but also pain and other motivations. The more I used this therapeutic implement, the more I realised that it helped me to find a silver lining in even the darkest emotions, experiences, observations and topics; find positivity even in the face of extreme negativity; find strength when I was being forced to feel weak; and find hope that my tomorrows would be brighter.

If you want to read some of my other poetry for free, then visit **followingwhispers.com** where you'll find my poetry blog (free email subscription available), plus details about my other books and social media presence.

Lastly, it would mean the World to me, if you left me an **honest book review** on the website or app where you purchased my book (Amazon, Kobo, Barnes and Noble, Apple Books, etc.). If you got this book from me directly, anywhere prestigious that it's for sale online (see above) will do. Small word-of-mouth gestures like this, help me more than you could ever imagine, so, thank you again for your time, love and support, I appreciate it ever so much.

Before You Go...

Recommended Checklist:

Leave me an **honest book review** online

Visit **followingwhispers.com**

Subscribe to my **free Poetry Blog** (if you haven't already).

Find out all about my other poetry books, by going to
followingwhispers.com/books

And last, but not least, reach out, **say hello**, and let me know which poems are your favourites, and why.

www.ingramcontent.com/pod-product-compliance
Lightning Source LLC
Chambersburg PA
CBHW071021080526
44587CB00015B/2444